I Love You to Pieces!

Barbara Benson Keith

Barbara Keith

Brownian Bee Press

For Pete...
I love you to pieces!

ISBN-13: 978-0-9789688-3-0
ISBN-10: 0-9789688-3-2

Summary: *I Love You to Pieces!* is a love story between animals and their babies. Owls, deer, pigs, rabbits, ducks and even whales express their parental love in this happy book, which features the mosaic artwork of Barbara Benson Keith.

Illustrations and text © 2014 by Barbara Benson Keith

Printed in Hong Kong

Published by Brownian Bee Press

Also by Barbara Benson Keith:
Mosaic Zoo: An ABC Book
The Girls and Boys of Mother Goose
Available at brownianbee.com

"I love you to pieces,
I love you so much!"
clucked the hen to her four little
chicks in the clutch.

"I love you to pieces,
I love you to bits!"
said papa fox to
his three little kits.

"I love you to pieces,
you bring me such joy!"
quacked mommy duck to
her good girls and boys.

"I love you to pieces,
you're my sweetie pie!"
said the sheep to her lamb
with a big happy sigh.

"I love you to pieces,
my dear little peanut,"
neighed the horse to her colt,
"and I really mean it!"

"I love you to pieces,
my rays of sunshine!"
Said the dog to her puppies,
"I'm glad you are mine!"

"I love you to pieces,
you do make me laugh!"
called papa whale to
his bright little calf.

"I love you to pieces,
my cute little pickle!"
cooed the deer to her fawn
as she gave him a tickle.

"I love you to pieces,
I'm under your spell!"
Armadillo told pups,
"Looks like I did well!

"We love you to pieces,
you're our honey bunch!"
said the owlets to mama,
beating her to the punch.

"I love you to pieces,
you're my little star!
My sweet calf, I love you,
just as you are!"

"I love you to pieces,
you all make me smile!"
said the croc to her hatchlings
as they sat by the Nile.

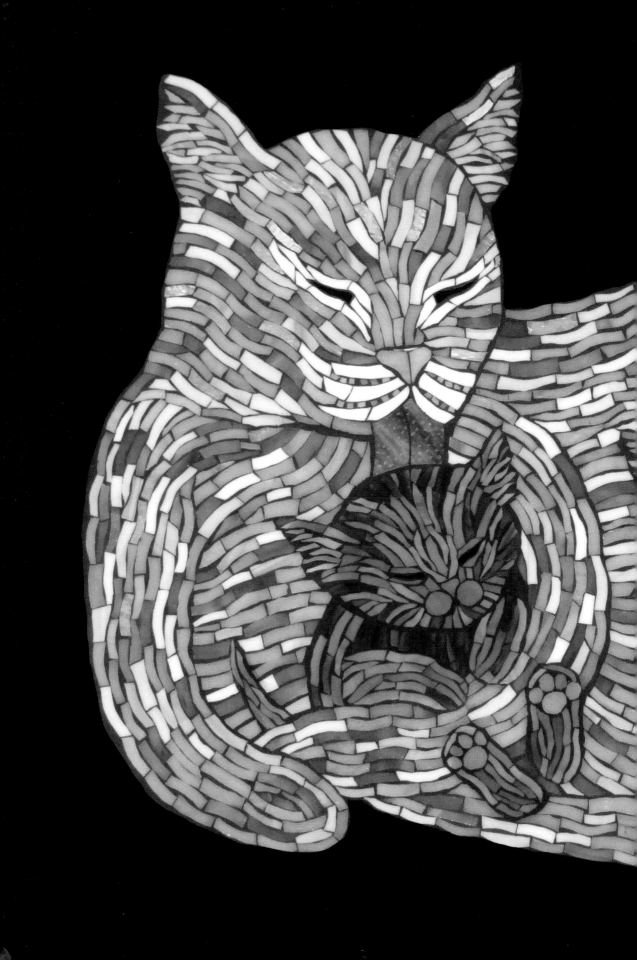

"I love you to pieces,
you're my snug-a-bugs!
Now, come here, my kittens,
for kisses and hugs!"

"I love you to pieces,
you're my funny honeys!"
said daddy rabbit
to six little bunnies.

"I love you to pieces,
you make my heart leap!"
squealed the pig to her piglets
as she sang them to sleep.

About the artwork...

The illustrations in this book are called mosaics. Mosaics are pictures that are made up of many smaller pieces. These mosaics were made out of stained glass. Some of the pieces have been painted with glass enamels and fired in a kiln, like these chicks.

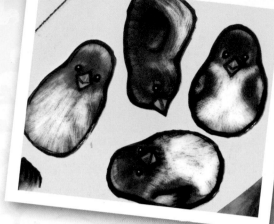

After I put the pieces of the mosaic together and glued them down to my board, I grouted the mosaic. The grout fills in all of the spaces between the glass pieces.

My next step was to photograph the mosaics and upload the images to my computer. In a photo editing program, I cut around all of the animals and brought them forward. Then I had a lot of fun editing the backgrounds, where I added patterns and shading, and I even changed some colors.

Not too long ago, I had received a note from someone telling me that they loved me "to bits". What a nice note to receive! The correlation this had to mosaics and also to my book inspired me. After all, what are mosaics, but lots of bits and pieces? Once I had the title, the verses flowed.

I hope you enjoy the final product—this book you are holding in your hands! Thank you so much for supporting the arts!

—Barbara Benson Keith